CW00365660

PREHISTORIC LIFE

Written by
John Malam

Illustrated by
John Butler, James Field,
Andrew Harland, Dud Moseley,
Stephen Sweet, Ross Watton

p

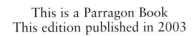

This is a Parragon Book
This edition published in 2003

Parragon
Queen Street House
4 Queen Street
Bath BA1 1HE, UK

Copyright © Parragon 2001

Original book created by

David West ☆ Children's Books

All rights reserved. No part of this publication may be reproduced, stored in a retrieval system, or transmitted by any means, electronic, mechanical, photocopying, recording or otherwise, without the prior permission of the copyright holder.

British Library Cataloguing-in-Publication Data

A catalogue record for this book is available from the British Library.

ISBN 1-40540-279-2

Printed in Dubai,U.A.E

Designers
Aarti Parmar
Rob Shone
Fiona Thorne
Illustrators
John Butler
Jim Eldridge
James Field
Andrew & Angela Harland
Colin Howard
Rob Jakeway
Mike Lacey
Sarah Lees
Gilly Marklew
Dud Moseley
Terry Riley
Sarah Smith
Stephen Sweet
Mike Taylor
Ross Watton
(SGA)
Ian Thompson
Cartoonist
Peter Wilks
(SGA)
Editor
James Pickering
Consultant
Steve Parker

CONTENTS

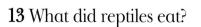

? How old is the Earth?

Earth is millions and millions of years old. In fact, our planet is four-thousand-six-hundred-million years old. When the Earth's age (4.6 billion years) is written as a number, it looks like this: 4,600,000,000. It's hard for us to imagine anything so old.

Earth today

 Amazing! Some of Earth's oldest known rocks are found in Scotland. They are about 3.5 billion years old.

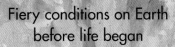
Fiery conditions on Earth before life began

? Has there always been life on the Earth?

Nothing at all lived on the Earth for the first billion (1,000 million) years of the planet's existence. The conditions were not right for life. There were no plants or animals of any kind. Earth was a dangerous place where life could not survive.

Has the Earth always looked the same?

200 million years ago

150 million years ago

80 million years ago

These maps show how Earth's land and sea looked in the past. To fit everything on them, Earth has been drawn as an oval. For a long time, all land was joined together in one giant mass. Over millions of years it broke up into smaller pieces. They turned into today's continents.

 Is it true?
The continents are still moving.

Yes. The continents move about 4 centimetres each year – the length of your little finger. Millions of years in the future, Earth will look very different from today.

? When and where did life on Earth begin?

Life on Earth began about 3.5 billion years ago. The first life appeared in the sea. It was born into a world that looked very different from today. The atmosphere was filled with poisonous gases. The sky was pink, and the sea was rusty-red.

Conditions on Earth were hostile when life first began.

Is it true?
Earth is the only planet with life on it.

Maybe. This is one of the greatest unsolved mysteries. Life probably does exist on other planets besides Earth, but nothing has been found so far. The search continues.

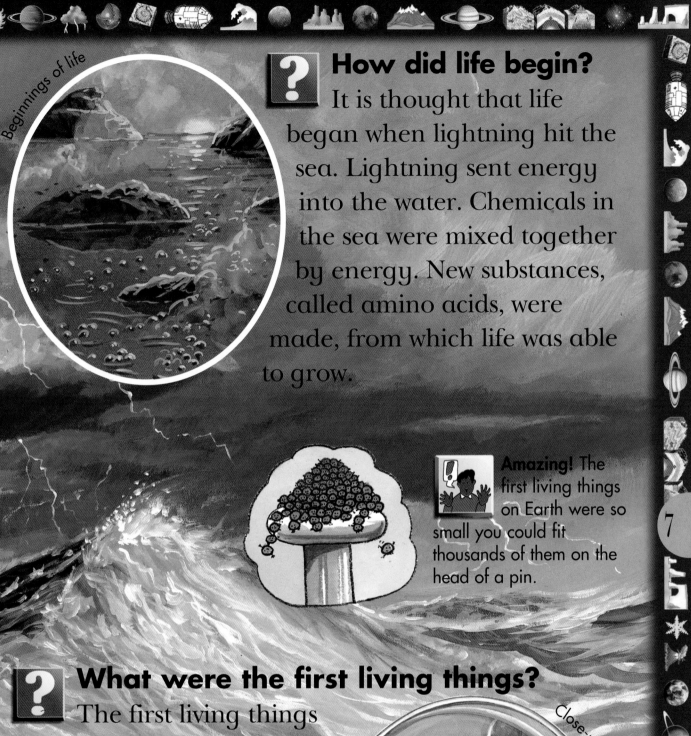

? How did life begin?

It is thought that life began when lightning hit the sea. Lightning sent energy into the water. Chemicals in the sea were mixed together by energy. New substances, called amino acids, were made, from which life was able to grow.

Amazing! The first living things on Earth were so small you could fit thousands of them on the head of a pin.

? What were the first living things?

The first living things were bacteria. They lived in the sea. Some bacteria changed into algae, which were simple plants. Algae lived in the sea in masses, like huge blankets. They made oxygen, which helped to turn the sky and sea blue.

Close-up of bacteria

What animals lived in the sea?

For millions of years all life lived in the sea. It was home to a huge variety of creatures, such as shellfish, worms, sponges and jellyfish. None of these animals had backbones.

Early sea life

Is it true?
The very first fish didn't have jaws.

Yes. Instead of jaws to open and close their mouths the very first fish sucked food into their mouths. They are called jawless fish.

Cladoselache (an early shark)

Acanthodians

Heliobatis fossil

Which animals first had backbones?

About 510 million years ago, new kinds of animals appeared in the sea. They were the first fish, and they were the first animals with backbones. Because they had backbones to support their bodies they could become much larger.

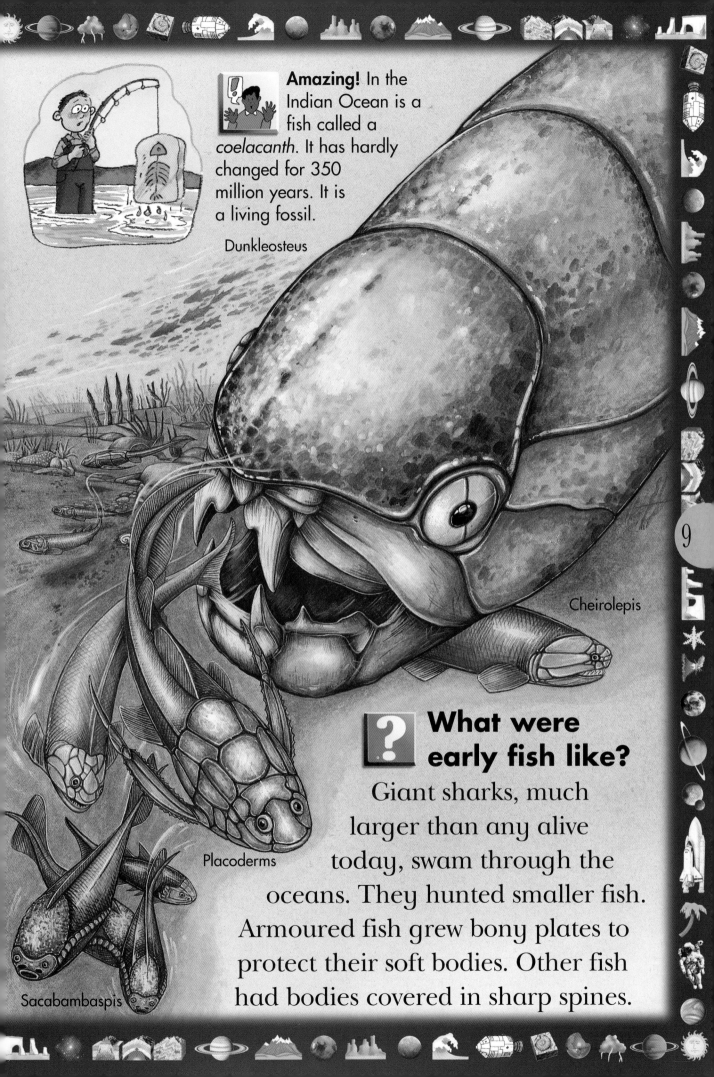

Amazing! In the Indian Ocean is a fish called a *coelacanth*. It has hardly changed for 350 million years. It is a living fossil.

Dunkleosteus

Cheirolepis

Placoderms

Sacabambaspis

? What were early fish like?

Giant sharks, much larger than any alive today, swam through the oceans. They hunted smaller fish. Armoured fish grew bony plates to protect their soft bodies. Other fish had bodies covered in sharp spines.

❓ When did life first appear on land?

About 440 million years ago, the first life appeared on land. It was simple plant life, similar to today's mosses. Then, about 400 million years ago, the first land animals – worms, spiders, scorpions and insects – evolved as they moved on to the land.

Is it true?
There are no amphibians alive today.

No. There are many different amphibians in the world today. Frogs, toads and salamanders are all amphibians.

Scorpion

Centipede

Cockroach

Why did some fish grow legs?

Some fish began to live in shallow water. It was difficult to swim in the shallows. To help these fish move around they grew short legs. Some of them also grew lungs, which meant they could breathe air. These animals could live in water and on land.

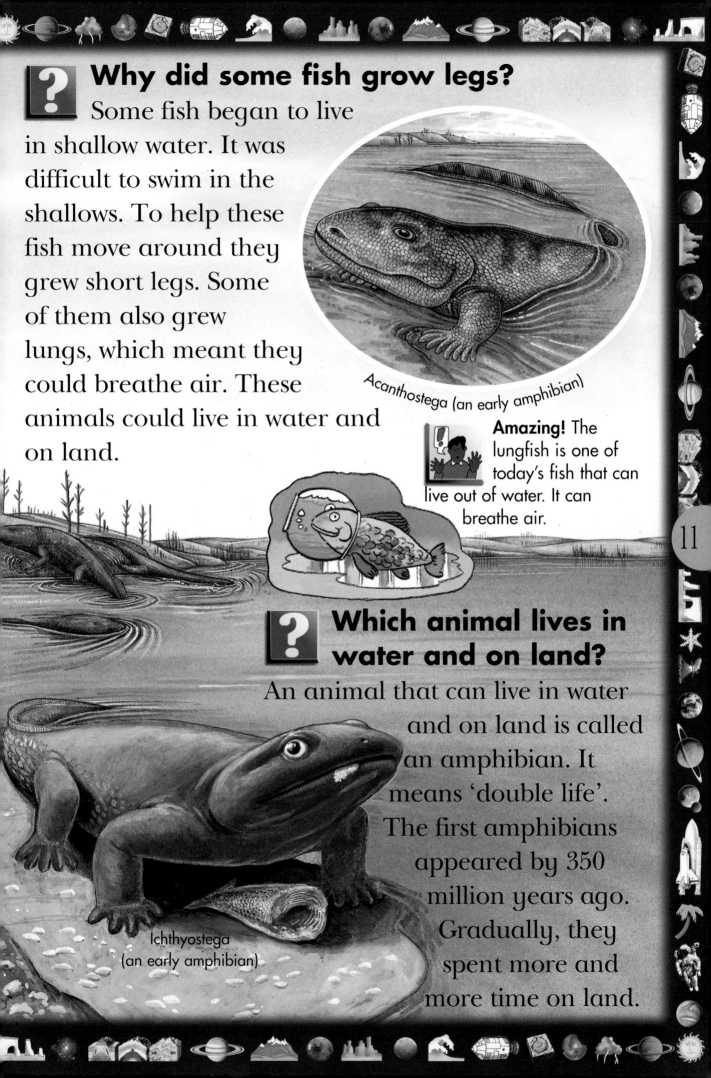

Acanthostega (an early amphibian)

Amazing! The lungfish is one of today's fish that can live out of water. It can breathe air.

Which animal lives in water and on land?

An animal that can live in water and on land is called an amphibian. It means 'double life'. The first amphibians appeared by 350 million years ago. Gradually, they spent more and more time on land.

Ichthyostega (an early amphibian)

? What are reptiles?

About 300 million years ago, some amphibians changed into reptiles. They could live on land all the time. Reptiles have backbones and scaly skin, and most lay eggs. Many reptiles, such as crocodiles, spend lots of time in the water, but they can't breathe underwater. They use the Sun to keep their bodies warm.

Is it true?
Some early reptiles had sails, on their backs.

Yes. *Dimetrodon* had a skin 'sail' on its back. It soaked up the Sun's heat, and controlled the animal's body temperature.

Hylonomus

What did reptiles eat?

The first reptiles, such as *Hylonomus*, were small lizard-like animals that ate tiny creatures. Reptiles learned how to run quickly so they could catch fast-moving insects. As reptiles became larger, they caught and ate bigger prey, including other reptiles. Some reptiles only ate plants.

Amazing! A small animal found in Scotland, in rocks that are 350 million years old, might be one of the first reptiles. But some scientists say it was an amphibian.

Hylonomus and dragonfly

Which reptiles had fur?

Some prehistoric reptiles grew fur on their bodies to keep themselves warm. These were the cynodonts. They lived about 245 million years ago. Over time they changed into a completely new group of animals, called mammals.

Cynognathus
(a cynodont)

Thrinaxodon
(a cynodont)

Crocodilian

Compsognathus

What were dinosaurs?
Dinosaurs were members of
the reptile family. They first
appeared about 225 million
years ago. For 160 million
years dinosaurs ruled the
Earth. They walked on straight
legs, tucked underneath their
bodies, and they lived on land.
The word dinosaur means
'terrible lizard'.

Hadrosaur
(a plant-eater)

Is it true?
*All dinosaurs
were big.*

14

No. The tiny
Compsognathus was
about the same size as
a chicken.

Deinonychus
(a meat-eater)

? What did dinosaurs eat?

Some dinosaurs were carnivores. This means they ate meat and fish. Some were herbivores. These dinosaurs ate plants. A third group were omnivores. They had a mixed diet and ate both meat and plants. Some dinosaurs swallowed stones, which crushed food inside their stomachs so it was easier to digest.

Seismosaurus
(a plant-eater)

Amazing! When *Ankylosaurus* filled its bony plates with blood it could have blushed pink!

15

? What colour were dinosaurs?

No one knows what colour dinosaurs were. Perhaps some had skins that matched their surroundings, making them hard to see. Some might have had bright markings to attract mates, or scare others away.

Tyrannosaurus rex and Hypsilophodons

Could dinosaurs make noises?

Dinosaurs had voice boxes, which means they could make noises. *Parasaurolophus* had a long, hollow bone on top of its head. Perhaps it forced air through the bone to make a deep, hooting sound.

Parasaurolophus

Amazing! A dinosaur has gone into space! In January 1998, a fossil *Coelophysis* skull travelled on board the space shuttle Endeavour. The 220-million-year-old fossil flew four million miles around the Earth.

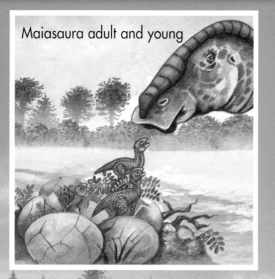
Maiasaura adult and young

? Did dinosaurs care for their young?

Yes, some did. *Maiasaura*, whose name means 'good mother lizard', cared for its young. Parents looked after them until they were old enough to take care of themselves.

Is it true?
Every animal on Earth died out with the dinosaurs.

No. Lots of animals survived. Birds, mammals, amphibians, insects, small reptiles (lizards), fish, spiders, snails and crocodiles all lived.

? Why did dinosaurs die out?

Dinosaurs died out 65 million years ago. Many people think this was because a big meteorite (a space rock) hit the Earth. It sent dust into the air which blotted out the Sun. Dinosaurs died because they were too cold and hungry.

Meteorite hitting Earth

Which creatures flew in the sky?

At the same time as dinosaurs walked on the land, other reptiles flew in the sky and swam in the sea. The sky reptiles were pterosaurs, which means 'winged lizards'. Their wings were not made from feathers, like a bird's, but from stretched skin.

Quetzalcoatlus

Liopleurodon

Which creatures swam in the sea?

The sea was home to many different reptiles. Some had very long necks. These were plesiosaurs, which means 'near lizards'. Others looked like today's dolphins. They were ichthyosaurs, which means 'fish lizards'. Ichthyosaurs were fast and agile swimmers.

Ichthyosaur

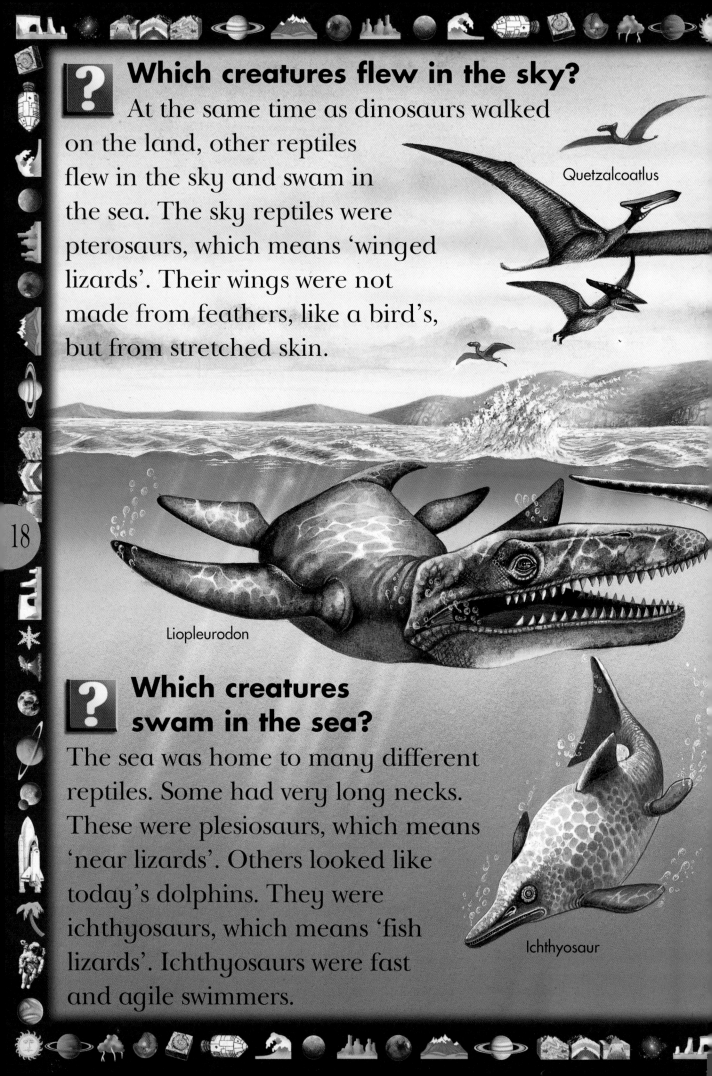

Pteranodon

Rhamphorhynchus

Plesiosaur

Feeding pterosaur

Is it true?
One pterosaur was as big as a small plane.

Yes. *Quetzalcoatlus* was an enormous pterosaur. It had wings 12 metres across. It is the biggest flying creature ever.

? What did pterosaurs eat?

Some pterosaurs ate fish, which they scooped from the sea with their long beaks. Some pterosaurs may have held lots of fish inside their cheek pouches, as pelicans do today.

Amazing! The short-necked plesiosaur *Liopleurodon* grew to 23 metres and weighed 50 tonnes. It was a giant sea monster!

19

❓ **What are birds?**

Birds are animals with backbones, they lay eggs, can make their own body heat, and have wings. They are also the only animals with feathers. Not all birds can fly. The first birds lived at the same time as the dinosaurs.

Prophaeton

Phororhacos

Is it true?
Ostrich eggs are the biggest eggs ever laid by a bird.

Hyracotherium
(a very small, early kind of horse)

No. The extinct bird *Aepyornis* laid the biggest eggs of all time. Each one was about the size of 150 hen's eggs.

❓ Where do birds come from?

Birds evolved from small, meat-eating dinosaurs. Fossils show that some of these dinosaurs had feathers. They are called 'dinobirds'. The first 'dinobirds' probably could not fly.

Caudipteryx

Amazing! Today's hoatzin bird, which lives in South America, has claws on its wings when young – just like *Archaeopteryx*, its prehistoric ancestor did.

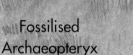
Fossilised Archaeopteryx

Archaeopteryx

❓ Which was the first true bird?

The first true bird – a bird that could fly – appeared about 150 million years ago. It is known as *Archaeopteryx*, which means 'ancient wing'. It had claws on its wings.

21

? What are mammals?

Mammals have backbones, their bodies are covered in hair or bristles, they make their own body heat, and they feed their young on milk. They have larger brains than most other animals.

Early mammals

Ginkgo tree

? When did the first mammals appear?

The first mammals appeared on Earth about 220 million years ago. They lived at the same time as the dinosaurs. Mammals survived after the dinosaurs died out, and then they became the ruling animals on Earth. There are about 4,200 different kinds of mammals alive today.

Did mammals only live on land?

Mammals came to live in all of Earth's habitats. Many lived on land, but some, such as bats, were able to glide through the air on wings of skin. Other mammals swam in the sea, such as whales, dolphins and seals.

Basilosaurus

Tyrannosaurus rex

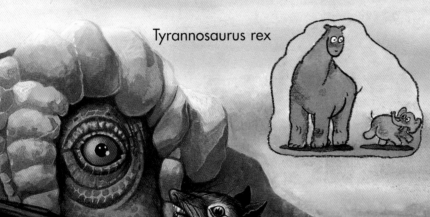

Megazostrodon

Is it true?
The elephant is the largest land mammal ever to have lived.

No. *Indricotherium* was the largest land mammal. It was almost 8 metres tall and as heavy as four elephants.

Amazing!
Woolly mammoths were big elephants with extra-long tusks up to 3 metres long. Their bodies were covered in fur.

Amazing! One *Australopithecus* is called Lucy. Her bones were found in 1974, when a song with the name Lucy in it was on the radio. She was named after it.

A group of human ancestors collecting fruit

Australopithecus skull

Who were our ancestors?

Our earliest ancestors were apes that walked upright on two legs. *Australopithecus*, meaning 'southern ape', was one of the first apes to walk upright. It lived at least three million years ago, and was short and hairy.

24

Yes. Compared with a modern human, an adult *Australopithecus* like Lucy was very short – about 1.2 metres tall.

? How did they live?

Australopithecus probably lived in small family groups. These bands of human ancestors wandered across the grassy plains of their homeland. They ate fruit, leaves, seeds and roots. They may have used sticks to help dig for food, and might have eaten meat, too.

25

AFRICA

Australopithecus finds

? Where did they live?

Australopithecus lived in Africa. Bones of this upright ape have been found in several countries, including Tanzania, Ethiopia and South Africa. Africa is where human species probably began, a few million years ago.

Homo
habilis

Homo
erectus

? Who were the very first humans?

The first people we think of as humans appeared in Africa. About two million years ago, *Homo habilis* (handy man) appeared. Then, more than one million years ago, *Homo erectus* (upright man) appeared, but they weren't modern humans.

Hand axe

Fire-making tool

Flint knife

? Did they have any tools?

Homo habilis was the first tool-user. This is why he is called 'handy man'. He made simple tools, such as choppers, from pebbles. The tools made by *Homo erectus* were better. He shaped stones into hand axes, and he was the first to use fire.

What did they eat?

Homo habilis and *Homo erectus* ate meat and plants. Meat probably came from dead animals which they found. They may have hunted for some small animals. Plants gave them berries and leaves. They used stone tools to cut and scrape their food.

Is it true?
Homo erectus was a wanderer.

Yes. More than one million years ago, *Homo erectus* began to move out of Africa, travelling to Europe and Asia.

Homo erectus people hunted and gathered their food.

Amazing! *Homo erectus* had fire. Fire provided warmth, gave heat for cooking, and offered protection from predators.

❓ When did modern humans appear?

Just over 100,000 years ago *Homo sapiens* appeared. The name means 'wise man'. They were modern humans. In Europe they lived during the freezing Ice Age, a time when glaciers covered the land. The Ice Age ended 12,000 years ago.

Mammoth hunt

Is it true?
Homo sapiens *have all died out.*

No. All people on Earth today are members of *Homo sapiens*. If they had died out, like other kinds of early human, none of us would be here today!

Where did they live?

Homo sapiens first appeared in Africa, and from there, they spread out across the world. They lived in cave entrances, and in places sheltered by overhanging rocks. In the open they made huts from branches, covered with skins.

As the climate grew warmer, Homo sapiens people migrated across the world.

Amazing! People who lived during the Ice Age played musical instruments. They made whistles from bones, and drums from shoulder-blades.

Animal carving

Cave painting

Were they artists?

The humans who lived in Europe during the Ice Age were among the first artists. They painted pictures of horses, bison and deer on the walls of their caves. Bone and ivory were carved into figures of animals and people.

How do we know about life in the past?

We find out about life in the past by looking for evidence. Fossils are one kind of evidence. They are the remains of living things that have been preserved. Objects made by humans, such as stone tools, are another kind of evidence.

A collection of fossils

Is it true?
Plants can't be fossilised.

No. Plants can become fossils, in the same way that animals can. By studying them we learn about the plants that once grew on Earth.

1

2

3

4

How is a fossil made?

It takes millions of years to make a fossil. The pictures on the left show how it happens. (1) An animal dies. Its body sinks to the bottom of a lake. (2) Sand and silt cover its body. (3) The flesh rots away. Minerals seep into the bones and turn them to stone. The animal is now a fossil. (4) The fossil is found.

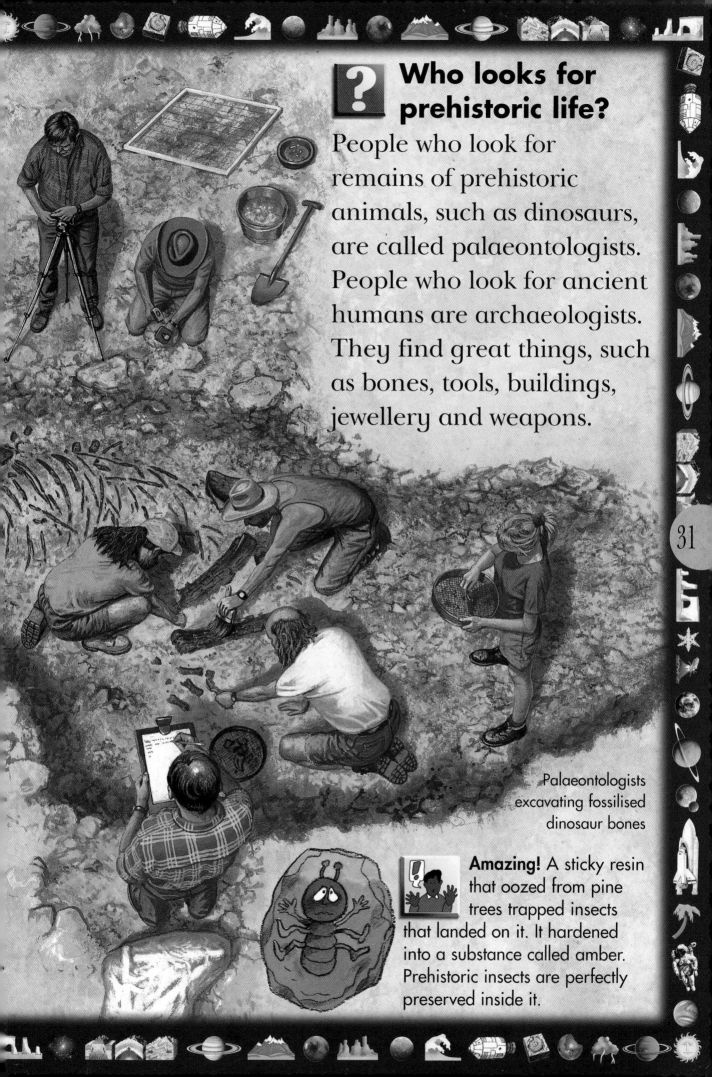

? Who looks for prehistoric life?

People who look for remains of prehistoric animals, such as dinosaurs, are called palaeontologists. People who look for ancient humans are archaeologists. They find great things, such as bones, tools, buildings, jewellery and weapons.

Palaeontologists excavating fossilised dinosaur bones

Amazing! A sticky resin that oozed from pine trees trapped insects that landed on it. It hardened into a substance called amber. Prehistoric insects are perfectly preserved inside it.

31

Glossary

Algae Tiny plants that live in water.

Amber Once liquid tree resin (sap) which has been fossilised.

Amphibian An animal that lives on land and in water, such as a frog.

Bacteria Tiny, living things that live in soil, water and the air.

Carnivore An animal that eats only meat.

Cynodont A type of reptile with fur, which evolved into mammals.

Dinosaur A type of reptile that once lived on Earth, but which has died out.

Fossil Remains of plants and animals from long ago.

Habitat The surroundings in which an animal lives.

Herbivore An animal that eats only plants.

Mammal An animal with a backbone that feeds its young on mother's milk.

Meteorite A space rock that hits the Earth.

Omnivore An animal that eats both meat and plants.

Oxygen A gas that animals breathe in and which keeps them alive.

Prehistoric An ancient time before writing was invented.

Prey An animal which is killed by another animal for food.

32

Index